Sabine Baring-Gould

A National Monument Of English Song

Sabine Baring-Gould

A National Monument Of English Song

ISBN/EAN: 9783741150876

Manufactured in Europe, USA, Canada, Australia, Japa

Cover: Foto ©Angelika Wolter / pixelio.de

Manufactured and distributed by brebook publishing software (www.brebook.com)

Sabine Baring-Gould

A National Monument Of English Song

English Minstrelsie

A National Monument of English Song

COLLATED AND EDITED, WITH NOTES AND
HISTORICAL INTRODUCTIONS, BY

S. BARING-GOULD, M.A.

THE AIRS, IN BOTH NOTATIONS, ARRANGED BY
H. FLEETWOOD SHEPPARD, M.A.
F. W. BUSSELL, B.D., Mus. B. Oxon.; AND
W. H. HOPKINSON, A.R.C.O.

IN EIGHT VOLUMES
VOLUME THE SIXTH

Edinburgh
T. C. & E. C. JACK, GRANGE PUBLISHING WORKS
1896

NOTES TO SONGS

VOL. VI.

𝕿𝖍𝖊𝖗𝖊 𝖎𝖘 𝖆 𝕱𝖑𝖔𝖂𝖊𝖗 (p. 1).—From "Maritana," by Wallace (William Vincent), of whom an account has already been given. Poor Wallace, whose life was not very happy and satisfactory, had a surprising power of evolving melody; he possessed real musical genius. His life was a series of experiments and failures. Now he was a violin-player, then lived in the bush in Australia, then he was in New Zealand, where he narrowly escaped being killed by the Maori, and did not get the sale and distribution that they deserved. Not being a trained musician, his airs lack form. John Percy died on Jan. 24th, 1797.

𝖂𝖊𝖑𝖑-𝖆-𝕯𝖆𝖞 (p. 6).—There was an old English ballad written on the death of Robert, Earl of Essex, who was beheaded on Ash Wednesday, 1601, that was sung to the air of "Well-a-Day."

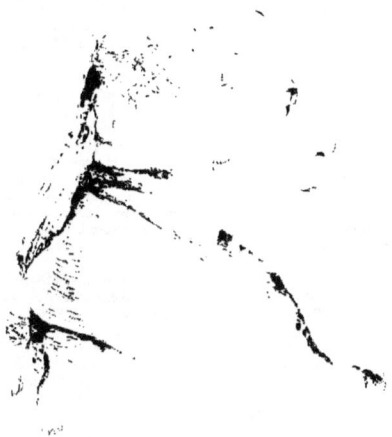

DR. SAMUEL ARNOLD.

was once saved in a most romantic manner by the chief's daughter. He died in 1865, in the Pyrenees, but his body was brought to England, and laid in Kensal Green Cemetery, attended by Balfe, Macfarren, Sullivan, and Sterndale Bennett. As the service closed, a robin-redbreast, from a tree hard by, poured forth a strain of song; it was the requiem of poor Wallace.

𝕾𝖜𝖊𝖊𝖙 𝕾𝖒𝖊𝖑𝖑𝖘 𝖙𝖍𝖊 𝕭𝖗𝖎𝖆𝖗 (p. 4).—A sonnet by Edmund Spenser, set to music by John Percy. It was given an accompaniment by Dr. John Clarke, who composed two volumes of vocal pieces to the words of Sir Walter Scott, the Ettrick Shepherd, Joanna Baillie, &c. Percy had no publisher. He issued all his compositions from his own private house, consequently, they

But the tune was older, for in 1566-7, one Wally had a licence to print "the second Well-a-Day," and in 1569-70, Thomas Colwell to print "a new Well-a-Day," that began "As plain, Mr. Papist, as Dunstable Way."

"To sing Well-away," says Mr. Chappell, "was proverbial even in Chaucer's time; for in the prologue to the 'Wife of Bath's Tale,' speaking of husbands, she says—

'I settle them so to werke, by my fay!
That many a night they sangen Weylaway.'

"And in the 'Shipman's Tale'—

'For I may synge, Allas! and Waylaway that I was born.'"

A

NOTES TO SONGS

Mr. Chappell gives one "Well-a-Day" in his "Popular Music of the Olden Time." That given here is another introduced by Dr. Arnold into the opera of "Zorinski." The air is certainly not by Arnold; it was probably traditional. The words of the opera were by Thomas Morton. It was performed at the Haymarket, in 1795. The song introduced into the play there has but one verse. I have made an addition. A third "Well-a-Day," modern and poor, is in the "British Orpheus," 1817; it begins—

"To the winds, to the waves, to the woods I complain."

Happy Land (p. 8).—By Dr. Rimbault, in 1837. The words by J. Bruton. Edward Francis Rimbault, son of Stephen Francis Rimbault, organist of S. Giles in the Fields, was born in Soho, in 1816. He became a pupil of Samuel Wesley, and at the age of sixteen was appointed organist of the Swiss Church, Soho. His special bent was in the direction of Old English music, and he was one of the founders of the Musical Antiquarian, and of the Percy Societies, of both which he was secretary. In 1841 he edited the publications of the Motett Society. In 1848 he received the honorary degree of LL.D. He will ever be remembered as one of the earliest and most enthusiastic students of Old English music. In 1850 he published "Musical Illustrations of Bishop Percy's Reliques of Ancient English Poetry." This was a collection of old ballad airs laboriously gathered from rare MSS. and early printed books. It was Rimbault who first drew Mr. Chappell's attention to the collections of Old English airs that were published early in the 17th century in Holland. Such are "Le Secret des Muses," Amsterdam, 1616; "Belerophon," ibid. 1626; "Triumphus Cupidinis," ibid. 1628.

Rimbault essayed his hand at an operetta, "The Fair Maid of Islington," 1838. A cantata, "Country Life," appeared after his death, in 1876. His song, "Happy Land," enjoyed extensive popularity, though it must be admitted to be feeble. Rimbault did a great work for English music, and it would not be right to leave him unrepresented in this work.

Give that Wreath to me (p. 11).—The words by T. Haynes Bayly; the tune is "Farewell to Manchester," composed in the early part of last century by the Rev. William Felton, prebendary of Hereford. It was originally part of one of his concertos, and was afterwards published under the title of "Felton's Gavotte." It is said to have been played by the troops of the Young Pretender in quitting Manchester, in December 1745. In 1746 it was printed as the music to a "Song on the Peace," that began—

"Fill, fill, fill the glass,
Briskly put it round;
Joyful news at last,
Let the trumpets sound.
Join with lofty strain,
Lovely nymphs, jolly swains:
Peace and plenty shall again
With wealth be crown'd."

Sir John Stevenson set Haynes Bayly's words to this air (1824). Felton was also the composer of the melody of "Bonny Bess, Sweet Blossom," in the Scottish style, that had a great run in the middle of last century. This also appeared in one of his concertos.

I am a Poor Shepherd Undone (p. 14).—This charming old song is in black-letter in the Douce Collection, and was printed by Richard Burton, at the Horse Shoe, in West Smithfield, 1641-74. It consists of fourteen stanzas, of which, as Mr.

Chappell points out, three have been appropriated and passed off as a Scotch song—"My father had forty good shillings."

The air went by another name, "Hey, ho, my honey!" because of a political song on the Parliament that was sung to the same melody. The tune is in "The Dancing Master," of 1665, in that of 1686, and in all later editions. It is in "Pills to Purge Melancholy," ed. 1719, vi. 284, three verses only.

The air was introduced into the "Beggar's Opera" for Polly Peachum's song, "When my hero in court appears."

There is a ballad in the Roxburgh Collection, "I am a poor man, God knows," that went to the same air. On the broadside copies the air is called "a West country tune."

Gather your Rosebuds (p. 16).—The words from the "Hesperides" of Robert Herrick, set by William Lawes, elder brother of the more famous Henry. He was son of William and probably nephew of Thomas Lawes, vicar-choral of Salisbury, and was a native of that city. At the expense of Edward, Earl of Hereford, he was given a musical education under Coperio. He was a member of the choir at Chichester, and was transferred, in 1602, to the Chapel Royal, and was afterwards one of the chamber musicians to Charles I. Fuller says that "he was respected and beloved by all who cast any looks towards virtue and honour." His gratitude and loyalty to his master were such that he took up arms in his cause, and, although, to exempt him from danger, Lord Gerard made him a commissary in the royal army, yet his zeal and energy made him face the enemy, and he was killed in the siege of Chester, in 1645.

In 1633, William Lawes composed the music to Shirley's "Triumphs of Peace." His songs and other vocal compositions appeared in "Select Musical Ayres and Dialogues," in 1653 and 1659; "Select Musical Ayres," 1652.

The air of "Gather your Rosebuds" is found in Playford's "Ayres and Dialogues," 1659, and in his "Introduction to Music," 3rd edition, 1660; and in "Musick's Delight on the Cithren," 1666; and in "The Musical Companion," 1667. The song is in "Merry Drollery Complete," 1670. Being arranged for three voices in Playford's "Musical Companion" for 1672, it became a favourite glee, and so was included in most glee books of the last century. It is in Forbes' "Cantus," 1682; and is included in the first volume of "The Essex Harmony," 1767.

When Lubin Sings (p. 18).—A song by John William Hobbs, born 1799, a chorister of Canterbury Cathedral. On reaching manhood his voice developed into a tenor of limited compass, but of remarkable purity and sweetness. He held a prominent position as a concert singer, and died in 1877. The song of "When Lubin Sings," the words by J. Gill, was published in 1842.

Begone, Dull Care (p. 20).—The words first appear in Playford's "Pleasant Musical Companion," Part II., 1687. It is found in many song books of last century, as "The Syren," 1737; "The Aviary," 1742; and "The Buck's Delight," 1793. The tune is derived from "The Queen's Jigg," which is in "The Dancing-Master" for 1701.

The song was given a new spell of life by its revival in the pantomime of "William Tell," at Sadler's Wells, 1793.

Originally the words ran "Begone, *old* care." The first time "dull" was substituted for "old" was in "The Buck's Delight."

The Stammering Lovers (p. 22).—A folk-song, taken down from an old mason on Dartmoor, in Devon. I have been unable to trace it. The humour of the song—such as it is—consists in the stuttering introduced in each verse. The air

NOTES TO SONGS

is in the Dorian mode, and is probably not later than the 16th century.

If Corn from Thee (p. 24).—A song from the "Amadigi" of Handel. Dr. Burney says—" As the music of 'Amadigi' was never printed, and his Majesty's score has been confided to my care for examination, the reader shall be made acquainted with the result." After saying what he thinks of the opera, he addresses himself to this song, and says, " This song, *se estinto è l'idol mio*, in my opinion is one of the best that Handel ever produced in his best style; the pathetic subject, the natural and pleasing imitations, the affecting modulation, and above all, the strain of sorrow which runs through every passage of the voice part, conspire to render it one of the most perfect compositions with which I have been acquainted."

This song was set to English words in Turle and Taylor's "Collection of Glees, Catches," &c., 1846, and it is from this that the present arrangement is chiefly taken.

We have come to consider Handel as our own, as his compositions were for English ears, and for the English stage and concert halls, and he wrote in England. There are many of his songs that might have been included in this collection. Those from " Acis and Galatea" have been purposely omitted, because they are so easily accessible in a cheap form.

Here's a Health unto His Majesty (p. 28).—This patriotic song, by Jeremiah Savile, first appeared in Playford's "Musical Companion," 1667, as a round. This was a very popular song in the reign of Charles II., and Shadwell mentioned it twice in his plays. In "The Miser," 1672, Timothy says, "We can be merry as the best of you—we can, i' faith—and sing *A bout, a bout (baste to the ferry)*, or *Here's a health to his Majesty, with a fa, la, la, lero*," and again, in " Epsom Wells," 1673, where Bisket says, "Come let's all be musitioners, and all roar and sing *Here's a health unto his Majesty, with a fa, la, la, la, lero*." By a strange mistake Savile has been called *Savage*. Savile composed songs for Playford's " Select Musical Ayres and Dialogues," 1653 ; he is now chiefly known by his four-part song, "The Waits," printed in Playford's "Musical Companion," which, by long standing custom, is the last piece sung at the meetings of the Madrigal Society.

Dr. Kitchener, in his " Loyal and National Songs of England," 1823, gives this song incorrectly. It will be noticed that this song is almost identical with "Once I loved a maiden fair," and that both are a reminiscence of the sixth Tone. In the original there is but a single verse. I have heard the song lately sung with a second—by whom written I do not know. As already pointed out, both are merely the 6th Tone in the first phrase. Chappell somewhat altered the second part of "Once I loved" from what is given by Playford in "The Dancing Master," 1650 ; &c. The original form has been given by Mr. Kidson in his "Country Dances."

The Miller of Dee (p. 30).—The complete song is found in "The Convivial Songster," 1782. Arne introduced one stanza into the opera of " Love in a Village," 1762 ; the play was by Bickerstaffe, but it can hardly be thought that he wrote the song. Had he taken the trouble to write one stanza he would probably have added others. The air is a robust old English melody, "The budgeon it is a delicate trade." The words of this latter song are in " The Triumph of Wit, or Ingenuity displayed," and in " A new Canting Dictionary, &c., with a complete collection of Songs in the Canting Dialect," 1725. A budge is a thief who steals clothes.

The tune was a favourite. It was introduced into several ballad-operas, as the "Quaker's Opera," 1728 ; " The Devil to Pay," 1731 ; "The Fashionable Lady," 1730, &c.

The air has been appropriated to the harvest supper song, " Here's a health unto our master," &c.

The tune was included by George Thomson, in 1824, in his collection of Scotch songs, harmonised by Beethoven, with a note in the index that the tune is English. It seems to have originated with the words at a period when a curious fashion set in for beggar plays and tales and songs. Of plays, " The Jovial Crew " was typical, by Richard Brome, 1641.

Love Will find out the Way (p. 32).—The words of this fine old song vary very considerably in different song books and collections. There is one version in Percy's " Reliques," another in Evans' "Old Ballads," 1810. A Third is in Rimbault's " Little Book of Songs and Ballads." Evans printed from a black-letter copy of the date 1620-28 ; Rimbault from Forbes' "Cantus," 1682 ; and Percy from a comparatively modern edition.

The ballad is quoted in Brome's "Sparagus Garden," 1635, and the burden, " Love will find out the way," was taken as title to a play in 1661.

A good many ballads were sung to this air, which is found in Playford's " Musick's Recreation on the Lyra Viol," 1652, in " Musick's Delight on the Cithren," 1666 ; and in " Pills to Purge Melancholy," 1719.

"The air is still current," says Mr. Chappell ; "for in the summer of 1855, Mr. Jennings, organist of All Saints' Church, Maidstone, noted it down from the wandering hop-pickers, singing a song to it, on their entrance into that town."

The air is not particularly good and original.

The song, " Love will find out the way," was carried into Scotland, and is reproduced in Scotch version in Johnson's " Musical Museum," but the tune is different.

Rest, Warrior, rest (p. 34).—This song was produced in 1811, in an historical play called "The Royal Oak," at the Haymarket. The songs in it were composed by Michael Kelly. "Connected with my recollections of this play," says he, "is an anecdote relative to my deceased friend, Lady Hamilton, so characteristic of that talented, but unfortunate woman, and at the same time so demonstrative of her warmth of feeling, that I cannot suffer it to pass unrecorded.

" I had composed a plaintive ballad in the second act for a Miss Wheatley, who possessed a fine, deep contralto voice—the poetry was descriptive of a warrior who had fallen in recent battle. Upon the fifth representation of the play, Lady Hamilton, with a party of friends, occupied one of the stage boxes, appearing all gaiety and animation. Scarcely, however, had this ballad commenced, when she became tremulous and agitated ; and at its conclusion, upon the *encore* being loudly demanded, she exclaimed, 'For God's sake remove me—I cannot bear it!' Her terrified friends withdrew her from the box, whence she was immediately conveyed home in a fainting condition.

"The following morning Miss Wheatley received a note from her ladyship, inviting her to her house, where, after complimenting her upon the great feeling with which she had given the melody, she added, 'The description brought our glorious Nelson with such terrible truth before my mind's eye, that you overwhelmed me at the moment, but now I feel as if I could listen to you in that air for ever.' She prevailed upon her visitor to repeat the ballad no less than four times at the pianoforte.

"Eventually, so powerful became this sentiment that she induced Miss Wheatley to retire from the stage altogether, and accept, under her roof, the post of musical governess to the young Horatio Nelson, who had been confided to her ladyship's guardianship. Not a day afterwards elapsed, but the favourite song was put in requisition. I

NOTES TO SONGS

published it under the title of 'Rest, Warrior, rest.' It was generally esteemed one of my happiest efforts."

Softly Rise, O Southern Breeze (p. 37).—This very fine air is by Dr. Boyce, and is taken from his oratorio of "Solomon," which was written by Edward Moore, and was produced in 1743. This tenor song, with bassoon obligato, long retained its popularity. William Boyce was the son of a cabinetmaker in London, and was born in 1710. He was articled under Dr. Maurice Greene, at St. Paul's Cathedral. Whilst still young, Boyce's hearing became impared, a serious trouble to him and hindrance in his profession as a musician.

He composed the music for Moses Mendez' little pastoral, " The

Bound Prentice to a Waterman (p. 42).—The words by William Cross. The music by James Sanderson. This English dramatic composer was born in 1769, at Workington, in the county of Durham, and from earliest childhood exhibited a dominating passion for music. When quite a little fellow he and his toy fiddle were inseparable companions. He was presented by his friends with a small violin, and learned the gamut from an old music-book, lent him by a dancing-master.

His father removed to Sunderland, and James Sanderson became acquainted with a violinist at the theatre, who took him into the orchestra, and allowed him to sit there at his side during the performance. The boy worked hard to improve himself, and in time was engaged at the theatre during the season, at a small salary.

DR. BOYCE.

(Drawn and Engraved by T. K. Sherwin.)

Chaplet," in 1750, which had a run, and was very popular, not on account of the merit of the piece and any poetry in it, but due to Boyce's fine music. Boyce is best known by his "Cathedral Music," a collection in score of the finest compositions for the Church of the English masters who preceded him. This was published in three volumes in 1760-78. Boyce died of gout in 1779.

Boyce composed a dirge for "Romeo and Juliet," and a similar piece for "Cymbeline," he also wrote music for the songs in "The Winter's Tale." Dr. Busby says of Boyce's compositions, "To peruse the melodies in his *Chaplet* and *Shepherd's Lottery*, is to be struck with the inventive playfulness of the most regulated imagination; examining the score of his *Solomon*, we look into a music of gold; but this allusion is not punctiliously complete, for all Boyce's gold is refined." We have already given his "Heart of Oak."

With his savings he bought himself an old spinet, and a book on the principles of thorough-bass, and at the age of fifteen was sufficiently accomplished to give lessons on the pianoforte and the violin. He then moved to Shields, where he earned a livelihood by giving lessons. At the end of three years he was engaged for the leadership of the orchestra at the theatre of Newcastle; but after twelve months, Astley, the proprietor of the Amphitheatre in London, carried him away, with the promise of an advanced salary. His first attempt at dramatic composition was at Chester, in 1789, when he composed symphonies to various parts of Collins's *Ode on the Passions*. His next work was the comic pantomime of "Harlequin in Ireland," 1792. From this date till 1820, he produced no less than one hundred and fifty-four melodramas, burlettas, pantomimes, &c., and received a salary of eight guineas a week as conductor at the minor theatres. He wrote a number of Vauxhall songs. His principal dramatic productions were "Black Beard," 1798, "Niobe," 1797, "Cora," 1799, "Sir Francis Drake," 1800, in which latter occurs the favourite song we now give. Indeed, this song "Bound Prentice" became a stock song that was introduced for half a century into most nautical plays, whenever a sailor came on the stage. Another favourite composition by Sanderson was "The Angling Duet," that was originally composed for "The Magic Pipe," an Adelphi pantomime. Sanderson died in or about 1841.

Somebody (p. 44).—This bright and pretty little song is found in "The British Musical Miscellany," 1805, "The British Orpheus," Stourport, *circ.* 1817, in "The Vocal Library," 1822, in Crosby's "Musical Repository," *circ.* 1810, "The Universal Songster," vol i., "The Edinburgh Musical Miscellany," vol. ii., 1793, and many others. There is a Scottish song, "For the sake of somebody," but it is different in words and in air. This latter appeared in Ramsay's "Tea-Table Miscellany" (1724), and was written by Allan Ramsay himself. The air was published in Oswald's "Caledonian Pocket Companion," *circ.* 1750. After that Robert Burns worked it up for the song, "My heart is sair, I daurna tell," &c., and this, with a rather different air, was printed in Johnson's "Scots Musical Museum," vol. v. This was frequently reprinted in Scotch collections. Another "Somebody," beginning, "O dearly I love somebody," was composed by Hook about 1800, and was sung by Mrs. Mountain at Vauxhall. The song we here give appears in Hyde's Collection, "harmonised by Mr. Webbe," vol. i., 1798; and on earlier engraved sheet-music, as "A favourite song and duet." I am much indebted to Mr. Kidson for information relative to this song. The character of the air is considerably earlier than the date at which it first appears in print associated to the little song of "Somebody."

A Jewel is My Lady Fair (p. 46).—Although not included in the "Orpheus Britannicus," the song is generally attributed to Purcell.

Advice to the Fair Sex (p. 49).—A song published by Falkener in his penny-a-page issues. It was sung by Mrs. Hudson at the gardens. The name of the composer is not known. R. Falkener, of 3 Peterborough Court and 45 Salisbury Court, Fleet Street, issued sheet music from type about 1775.

Shepherds, have you seen my Pastora? (p. 52).—This is an old Vauxhall song, the composer and author unknown.

I Dreamt that I Dwelt in Marble Halls (p. 54).—From the favourite opera of "The Bohemian Girl," words by Bunn, music by Balfe.

Fitzball, in his egoistical, but amusing "Thirty-five Years of a Dramatic Author's Life," thus describes the advent of Balfe in England:—

"Balfe, whose early musical works had brought him, on the Continent, a considerable reputation, wished to compose an opera for Mr. Arnold, lessee and manager of the English opera, for England. It was Mr. Arnold's equal desire that he should do so. A poet was in request : I was the person made choice of. To Mr. Arnold I was entirely a stranger. Balfe had never heard of me, nor I of him.

"My first interview, both with Mr. Arnold and Mr. Balfe, was in Mr. Arnold's room in the theatre. A subject for this opera was wanting. At length 'Linda de Chamouni' was suggested, I think by Balfe. Although I was acquainted with the work, strange to say, having read it a few days previously, with no very great relish for its beauties—one of my systems being never to throw what is called a wet blanket over the suggestions of genius—I immediately adopted the story, rechristening it under the name of 'The Siege of Rochelle.' I set to work with an ardour and vigilance for which I was then celebrated. In a day or two the first act was complete, and Balfe hammering away, as he could hammer, at his pianoforte. Piece after piece of music flowed, like rich argosies, into the theatre; copyists were set to work, parts distributed, everything conduced to bid fair for the production of Balfe's first English opera at the English Opera House."

As it happened, however, the performance took place not where first intended, but at Drury Lane.

"It was a glorious night, the first night of 'The Siege of Rochelle,' one to wish your whole life long the first night of a new play or a new opera. The cram there was, the fashion, the delicious music, the enthusiastic applause, the double encores—never had I witnessed anything like it! 'Vive le Roi!' 'Lo! the early hours of morning,' and 'When I beheld the anchor weighed,' were especial marks of approbation, and had an immense sale at the publishers. The applause was unanimous. So carried away were even persons of the highest consequence by the enthusiasm created by this beautiful music (thought by many still to be Balfe's best composition), that people bent over and nearly threw themselves from the side boxes, next to the orchestra, to congratulate and shake hands with the young composer. They crowned him with a wreath of flowers, and I question, amid all the numerous and brilliant successes of this great artist (Balfe), if he ever felt such a delighted heart as on the first night of 'The Siege of Rochelle.' It ran nearly the whole season; and the first time her present gracious Majesty went in state to the theatre, it was to the Theatre-Royal, Drury Lane; 'The Siege of Rochelle' being performed by special desire. There is a celebrated portrait of her Majesty, by Paris, seated in the box."

The Pilot (p. 57).—A well-known song by Sidney Nelson; the words are by T. Haynes Bayly.

Here's a Health to the Lass (p. 60).—A very favourite drinking-song during the last century, but the original words are not such as would bear singing now-a-days. The words, accordingly, have been considerably toned down. Amongst other collections that contain this song may be named "The Convivial Songster," 1782. It appears somewhat earlier in half-sheet engraved music, not earlier than 1770.

Let Ambition Fire the Mind (p. 61).—Sung by Juno in William Congreve's masque of "The Judgment of Paris," in 1701, and performed at the theatre in Dorset Gardens. The music was by Weldon. We have already given this air as used in duet form in "Love in a Village," between a soprano and contralto. We have thought it advisable to give it here again as a Tenor solo, to the original words. Congreve, in a letter to a friend, dated March 26, 1701, says—"I don't think any one place in the world can show such an assembly. The number of performers, besides the verse-singers, was eighty-five. The front of the stage was all built into a concave with deal boards, all which are faced with tin, to increase and throw forward the sound. It was all hung with sconces of wax candles, besides the common branches of lights usual in the play-houses. The boxes and pit were all thrown into one, so that all sat in common; and the whole was crammed with beauties and beaux, not one scrub being admitted. The place where formerly the music used to play, between the pit and stage, was turned into White's chocolate-house, the whole family being transplanted thither with chocolate, cooled drinks, ratifia, pasties, &c., which everybody that would called for, the whole expense of everything being defrayed by the subscribers."

The song appears on early half-sheets as sung by "Juno in the Prize." The reason of this is, that a prize of £200 was offered for the best music for Congreve's Masque. Daniel Purcell and Eccles competed with Weldon, but the latter obtained the prize. Mr. F. Kidson is in possession of a very rare folio copy of Daniel Purcell's compositions, and in this occurs his setting of "Let ambition fire thy mind."

In duet form it is given in the "Essex Harmony," vol. i., *circ.*, 1786.

Arne recast the music of the Masque by Congreve in 1740, and then wrote a fresh air, a very inferior tune, which may be found in "Clio and Euterpe," 1758. Dr. Burney says of Weldon's composition, that "the melody is so natural and pleasing that, like an evergreen in vegetation, it will always be fresh and in season."

John Weldon died in 1736.

"Let ambition fire thy mind," sung as a solo, as an address of Juno to Paris, is bold and rhythmic in form.

The Diver (p. 64).—Words by G. Douglas Thompson, the music by G. J. Loder, who was born at Bath in 1813, and died in 1865. Mr. Husk says of him—"His compositions are distinguished by the melodiousness of the parts, and their skilful instrumentation."

I have a Silent Sorrow (p. 68).—The lines were the composition of R. B. Sheridan, and the air was that of Georgiana, Duchess of Devonshire. She was the daughter of John, first Earl Spencer, and was born in 1774. She married William Cavendish, fifth Duke of Devonshire, and died in 1806. This song was published in 1798. It had been arranged for her, with pianoforte accompaniment, by Shaw. It was introduced into "The Stranger," an adaptation of a play of Kotzebue, and sung by Mr. Bland, 1798.

Phillis on the New-Mown Hay (p. 70).—The ballad is in the Roxburghe Collection. The tune is that of "Amarillis told her swain," which is in "Merry Drollery Complete," 1670. The air is given in "The Dancing-Master" of 1665, and in all the later editions; in "Musick's Delight on the Cithren," 1666; in "Apollo's Banquet," 1670; and in "The Pleasant Companion for the Flageolet," 1680. Other songs were set to the air, as "Love in the Blossom," and "The Cotsall (Cotswald) Shepherds."

The Cheshire Cheese (p. 72).—A robust Cheshire folksong, first published by Edward Jones in his "Popular Cheshire Melodies," 1798. Jones did good service in collecting Welsh melodies, but he included among those he published some of demonstratively English origin. This song has been republished in Miss Broadwood's "Country Songs," 1895.

The Mermaid (p. 74).—Mr. Chappell was the first to publish the folk-air to which this very favourite song of the people is sung. He had it from a Mr. Charles Sloman, and it was fastened on by G. A. Macfarren, and by B. Roefs, both in 1868, and published as a song with their settings.

The song is really a long ballad; it is found in broadside in "The Sailor's Caution," Peterhead, c. 1815; in "The Glasgow Lasses' Garland," and in "The Sailing Trade Garland," (Garlands, Brit. Mus., 11,621; b. 13; c. 3). Chappell and his followers give six stanzas only. In reality there are many more. The various printed editions differ, and singers among our peasantry to this day give, some more and some less. I have often heard it from old song-men in the West of England. The song and air are also traditionally known in Yorkshire. As the complete ballad is not generally known, I give it here in its entirety, as far as can be recovered:

As we lie musing on our beds,
So well and warm at ease,
O little do we rack our heads
For the sailors on the seas.
O the raging seas do roar,
And the stormy winds do blow,
While we poor sailors go up aloft,
And the landsmen lie down below.

We do endure both hot and cold,
And many bitter blasts,
And oftentimes we too are told
To cut away our masts;

And overboard our guns to throw,
And many a cargo brave,
And in the long-boat forced to go,
Our precious lives to save.

On Friday morn as we set sail,
We were not far from land,
O then we spied a fair pretty maid,
With a comb and glass in hand.

The first came up was the mate of our ship,
With line and lead in hand,
To sound and see how deep was she
From any rock or sand.

The next came up was our boatswain,
Of courage stout and bold.
Stand fast, stand fast! till the danger's past.
Stand fast, my hearts of gold!

Our gallant ship is gone to wreck,
Which late so well was trimm'd;
The raging sea has sprung a leak,
And the salt water runs in.

Our gold and silver, and eke our clothes,
And all that e'er I have,
We overboard constrained throws,
Thinking our lives to save.

In all the numbers then on board,
'Twas five hundred sixty-four,
But all alive were ninety-five
That ever reached the shore.

The first up spoke the good captain,
And a well spoken man was he.
I have a wife in Plymouth town,
And this night a widow she'll be.

The next up spoke the gallant mate,
And a well spoken man was he.
I have a wife in Portsmouth town,
And this night a widow she'll be.

The next up spoke the good boatswain,
And a gruff-spoken man was he.
I have a wife in fair Exeter,
And this night a widow she'll be.

The next up spoke the little cabin-boy,
And a pretty little boy was he.
I am as sorry for my mother dear,
As are you for your wives three.

Last night when the moon shone bright,
My mother sons had five,
But now look may she in the salt, salt sea,
And find but one alive.

NOTES TO SONGS vii

Call a boat, call a boat, you little Plymouth boy,
    Dost hear the wild sea sound?
For the want of a boat wherein to float,
    Our merry men most were drowned.

O three times round went our gallant ship,
    O three times round went she,
And down in the wave, where none might save,
    She sank to the bottom of the sea.

𝔗𝔥𝔢 𝔅𝔞𝔫𝔨𝔰 𝔬𝔣 𝔄𝔣𝔣𝔞𝔫 𝔚𝔞𝔱𝔢𝔯 (p. 77).—Words by M. G. Lewis, the air by "A Lady." The date of this song is about 1820. Mr. Frank Kidson, in a communication to the *Leeds Mercury Supplement*, April 14, 1894, after having mentioned that Lewis was

a-wooing go." In Power's list of new songs, "Banks of Allan Water" is found with Horn's name attached, also under "Glees," with the name of Wm. Hawes, and under "Pianoforte Solos" that of Chipps. This indicated that while the melody itself was the composition of the mysterious Lady of title, C. E. Horn was the arranger and harmoniser of it in the song form, as were Hawes in the case of the glee, and Chipps in that of the pianoforte solo. The "Allan Water" that Lewis immortalises is, I believe, that near Stirling, and near where the Bridge of Allan stands, or did ten years ago, an old mill on its banks, which those who like to do can fancy as the home of the ill-fated girl."

𝔑𝔬 𝔉𝔩𝔬𝔴𝔢𝔯 𝔱𝔥𝔞𝔱 𝔅𝔩𝔬𝔴𝔰 (p. 80).—From "Selima and

THOMAS HAYNES BAYLY.
(*From an Engraving by C. Cook in the British Museum.*)

the writer of the words, says:—"It is possible that Lewis wrote the song "The banks of Allan Water" to the very old Scottish air, "Allan Water," though I confess I can find no record of its having been sung to that air. The tune we now know was set to the song shortly before the author's death, and was first published by J. Power (Thomas Moore's musical publisher), about the year 1815, in a folio sheet, "the words by M. G. Lewis, Esq., composed by Lady ———." Later, in one of Power's publications for the flute, "Minstrel Lays," the composer's name is more fully hinted at as "Lady C. S.," but who this lady was I have not been able to ascertain. The air has been ascribed to C. E. Horn, and it is much in his style. He was the composer of "I've been roaming," and other popular favourites, including his best-known air to that nursery favourite, "A frog he would

Azor," acted at Drury Lane, 1776. The play was borrowed and altered from a French original, and the bulk of the music was by Grétry. The alteration was made by Sir George Collier, but it was a poor play, and was only saved from being hissed by the charming singing of Mrs. Baddely. The song we give was composed by Thomas Linley, the father of Sheridan's accomplished and charming wife.

𝔍 𝔭𝔯𝔞𝔶 𝔗𝔥𝔢𝔢 𝔰𝔢𝔫𝔡 𝔐𝔢 𝔅𝔞𝔠𝔨 𝔪𝔶 𝔥𝔢𝔞𝔯𝔱 (p. 84).— The words by Sir John Suckling, and the air by Edward Miller, in 1756, organist of Doncaster. He was born at Norwich in 1731, and was the son of a pavior, who brought him up to the same trade; but the lad ran away to learn music, and studied under Dr. Burney. He died at Doncaster in 1807, at the age of seventy-six, after having been organist of Doncaster parish church for fifty years. He not only composed songs and glees and psalm tunes, but was also the author of a "History of Doncaster," that is still in repute. Sir John Suckling was born in 1613, and died at the age of twenty-eight, in 1641. His song, "Why so pale and wan, fond lover?" is perhaps his best known composition; and the delightful ballad, "I'll tell thee, Dick, where I have been," is a delicious picture of a wedding in the seventeenth century.

Encompassed by an Angel's Frame (p. 86).—From General Burgoyne's play of "The Lord of the Manor," acted at Drury Lane, 1781. The music was by William Jackson of Exeter. This song was admitted into "Knight's Musical Library," one of the first, if not the first, attempt at giving the public a serial of cheap popular music.

In the memoirs of a "Gentlewoman of the Old School," is the following pleasant account of Jackson:—

"There was a musical party in the town, taught by the celebrated W. Jackson of tuneful memory. He used to indulge in private meetings, that is, with four or five of his best scholars, when they sung canzonets, elegies, &c., chiefly Jackson's compositions, who always accompanied on the instrument, and with his fine deep bass voice. Handel's music was also played and sung, and a harpsichord, with a double row of keys, for that composer's works, was preferred, although pianofortes had come to light and sound, but not with those strong powers they now possess. I was the only one not a performer allowed to be present, because I could hold my tongue and snuff the candles; and never was a person more delighted at hearing what it might be supposed I could not understand; but harmony reaches all hearts that have feeling, and to this day I recollect 'Time has not thinn'd my flowing hair,' and 'In a vale closed with woodlands.'

"Jackson was a man of sense and talent, did not paint badly, made good sketches, had read much, and conversed very agreeably. One inconvenience attended him not uncommon in his profession; he had a very nice ear, and not being of a sordid disposition, and his compositions having had a very extensive sale at home and abroad, especially in Italy (so that he was in easy circumstances), he resolved on trying the experiment of teaching only those who were likely to play well, and thus save his own ears and his employers' purses. I knew a lady to whom he said, 'I cannot any longer pick your pocket, your daughter will never play.' He attended a family in the neighbourhood one whole day in the week, for which he received £100 a year, equal to £200 at present; there were several daughters who did credit to the instruction they received; but the father of the family wished to be a musician, and asked Jackson whether, if he took lessons on the violoncello, he should be able to play? 'No, never, give me leave to tell your Lordship.' Need I say the honest man was dismissed, and another master supplied his place."

As I Saw Fair Clora Walk (p. 88).—A duet by George Hayden, organist of St. Mary Magdalen's Church, Bermondsey. He composed and published three cantatas in 1723. He also was the composer of a "New Mad Tom," commencing, "In my triumphant chariot hurled," which was afterwards tacked on to the former part of the older song, "Forth from my dark and dismal cell," in place of the latter verses, beginning, "Last night I heard the dog-star bark."

Long Long Ago (p. 92).—Certainly Haynes Bayly was a master in his peculiar line—that of sentimental song. He was the forerunner of the composers of that whole series of namby-pamby stuff which has an enormous run at the present day. But his compositions were superior to what has followed; and some of his best songs, words and music, will not die, when all the later stuff has perished in the dust-heap.

Old Ringwood (p. 94).—A favourite hunting song, the poetry by Robert Blomfield, and the air by William Hawes, who was born in London in 1785, and was a chorister of the Chapel Royal from 1793 to 1801. In 1802 he was engaged as a violinist for Covent Garden Theatre. In 1805 he was appointed gentleman of the Chapel Royal, and in 1814 vicar-choral of St. Paul's Cathedral. In the same year he became lay-vicar of Westminster Abbey, but resigned in 1820. He carried on business for some years as a music-seller in the Strand, and was director of the music at the Lyceum. It was at his instance that Weber's "Der Freischütz" was produced in England, July 24, 1824; and this marked an epoch in the history of the opera in England. Hitherto the public would tolerate nothing but the modest ballad operas, and grand operas in Italian; "Der Freischütz" was ventured on with

W. Hawes.

great timidity, and Hawes did not at first dare to give this great work in its integrity. However, it proved a success, and this encouraged him to adapt a large number of foreign operas to the English stage, such as Winter's "Interrupted Sacrifice," Mozart's "Cosi fan Tutte," and Marschner's marvellous creation, "The Vampire." He also compiled music for many operas that appeared between 1829 and 1839. He was a composer of glees and madrigals, and he edited "The Triumphs of Oriana," a collection of old English madrigals. He died in 1846, and it must not be forgotten that, although he composed little of superior quality, nevertheless he laboured hard, and achieved much in the elevation of English musical taste. His gifted daughter, Maria Billington Hawes, afterwards Mrs. Merest, has bequeathed some very delightful songs, that have, perhaps, more melodious merit than anything composed by her father.

Let me Wander not Unseen (p. 96).—The words by Milton, and the music by Handel. This air was employed for the song "My Dolly," in "Love in a Village," 1762. The words are—

"My Dolly was the fairest thing,
   Her breath disclosed the sweets of spring,
And if, for summer you would seek,
   'Twas painted in her eye and cheek;
Her swelling bosom, tempting ripe,
   Of fruitful autumn was the type;
But when my tender tale I told,
   I found her heart was winter cold."

The lines of Milton's are, with a slight alteration, from "L'Allegro," "Sometimes walking not unseen." Handel composed the cantata in 1740, but revised it the following year. "Let me Wander" found its way in "The Universal Harmony," 1745, and many other collections.

They Tell Us (p. 98).—From Purcell's "Indian Queen." The song is also published in the second volume of his "Orpheus Britannicus," p. 59.

Mr. Husk writes of Purcell's music:—"Purcell essayed every species of composition. He wrote for the Church, the theatre, and the chamber. . . . His secular music displays his imaginative faculty, his singular dramatic instinct and skill in marking character, his rare gift of invention, and great powers of expression. Although, viewed by the light of our own day, his instrumental chamber compositions appear of an inferior order, they will yet, when compared with those of his predecessors and contemporaries, be found greatly in advance

of his time. We see in him the improver of our cathedral music; the originator of English melody, as the term is now understood; the establisher of a form of English opera which was almost universally adopted for upwards of a century and a half; the introducer of a new and more effective employment of the orchestra in accompaniment; the man who excelled all others in his accurate, vigorous, and

energetic setting of English words; and the most original and extraordinary musical genius that our country has produced. It is hardly possible to estimate the loss to English art by the early death of Henry Purcell. Had his life been prolonged for him to have witnessed the introduction into England of the Italian opera, and the

early career in this country of Handel, what might not have been expected of him?"

Through the kindness of Mr. F. Sherlock, I am able here to reproduce, from "The Church Monthly," the coat-of-arms of Purcell, showing his arms impaled with those of Petre of Torbrian,

NOTES TO SONGS

Devon, as also a picture of his monument in Westminster Abbey; further, a specimen of his musical notation, being a portion of the Te Deum and Jubilate for St. Cecilia's Day, 1604.

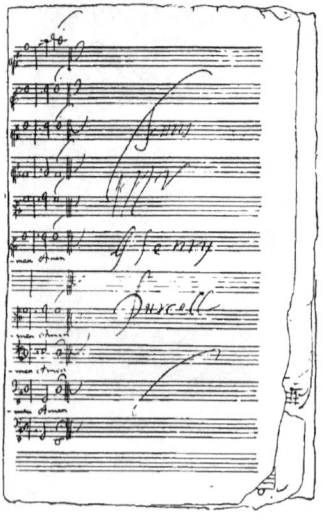

George Ridler's Oven (p. 100).—Found in "Abstracts of the Records and MSS. respecting the County of Gloster," by Thomas Dudley Fosbroke, F.S.A., 1802. Dixon gives this song in "Ballads of the Peasantry of England," published for the Percy Society—afterwards republished by Robert Bell; he says that it is an old Gloucestershire song, sung at the annual dinners of the Gloucestershire Society from the earliest period of its existence (1657). In 1776 there was a Harmonic Society at Cirencester, which always opened its meetings with "George Ridler's Oven" in full chorus. The annual meeting is held at Bristol in August, where the members dine, and this song is sung; the late Duke of Beaufort was wont to lead off the glee in capital style. It is stated that the words have a secret meaning, well-known to the members of the Gloucestershire Society, which was originally composed of strict Royalists. By George Ridler, Charles I. was meant, and the "Oven" was the Cavalier party. But all this is absurd. What seems clear enough is, that it is a simple folk-song relative to a certain George Ridler, who built an oven of Blakeney stone from the Forest of Dean. There is a comical touch in making the eldest son take the bass *because* he is the first born. The entire ballad consists of eight stanzas, of which three consist of the song sung in accordance with George Ridler's boast. This song is the well-known old "My dog and I," and the verses run thus—

"My hostess's maid, her name was Nell,
A pretty wench, and I loved her well;
I loved her well, good reason why,
Because she loved my dog and I.

My dog is good to catch a hen;
A duck or goose is good for men;
And where good company I spy,
O thither goes my dog and I.

My dog has gotten such a trick
To visit maids when they be sick;
When they be sick and like to die,
O thither goes my dog and I."

This song of "My Dog and I" in its entirety is in the Roxburgh Collection. The air to which "George Ridler's Oven" is sung is the same as the Gloucestershire Wassailers' song, says Mr. Chappell, in his edition of 1838, No. 212. As "My Dog and I" is an interesting and curious song I give it also, a little later in this volume.

Mr. Hughes gives this song in the "Scouring of the White Horse."

The "My dog and I" exists in two forms. One in the Roxburghe Collections was sung to the air of "Lavender blue, lavender green," the other to "Bobbing Joan."

The words will be found in "The New Olio," 1791.

There is in "George Ridler's Oven" a verse that has a certain similarity to the Scotch song, "When I have sixpence under my thumb," but it does not in the smallest degree follow that in George Ridler there is any reminiscence of a Scotch song, but that both derive from an original common throughout England and the Lowlands of Scotland. Through the kindness of Mr. Kidson I have been furnished with a setting of "George Ridler's Oven," taken down by himself, from a Gloucestershire singer, about 1880.

The tune "Lavender blue, lavender green," lingers on as a nursery air, and is given in Walter Crane's "Baby's Opera," p. 17. There the words are—

"Lavender's blue, diddle, diddle! Lavender's green;
When I am king, diddle, diddle! you shall be queen,
Call up your merry men, diddle, diddle! I set them to work,
Some to the plough, diddle, diddle! some to the cart;
Some to make hay, diddle, diddle! some to cut corn;
While you and I, diddle, diddle! keep ourselves warm."

Adieu to the Village Delights (p. 102).—Composed by Lord Littleton upon the death of his wife, Lucy, daughter of Hugh Fortescue of Filleigh, Esq., who died 19th January 1746-7. He had been deeply attached to her, and their marriage was but of short duration. The music was by Joseph Baildon.

William Gardiner, in his "Music and Friends," 1838, says that, in 1771, on the Sunday previous to the opening of the new Infirmary at Leicester, when there was a gathering of county notabilities, his father dined at Gumley Hall, with Mr. Cradock, Lord Sanderson, and others. On the cloth being drawn, his Lordship called for catch-books, and started Lord Mornington's catch—

"'Twas you, sir,
'Twas you, sir, that kiss'd the pretty girl ;
'Twas you, sir, you."

But Mr. Gardiner, who was a strict Presbyterian, thinking this very unsuited to Sunday, when it came to his turn, sang "Adieu to the Village Delights," as being more consonant with the sacredness of the day. On the ladies retiring, Mrs. Cradock, in passing Mr. Gardiner's chair, took occasion to express her approbation of his choice.

Joseph Baildon, the composer, flourished between 1760 and 1780. He was lay-vicar of Westminster Abbey, and in 1766 gained a prize for his fine glee, "When gay Bacchus fills my breast." He published a collection of songs in two books, entitled "The Laurel," and "Four favourite Songs sung by Mr. Beard at Ranelagh Gardens."

"Adieu to the Village Delights," though composed as a glee, was very generally sung as a song.

Oh, forbear! (p. 104). A song, the words by Aaron Hill, and the air by Abiel Whichello. A more famous song, composed by Whichello, was "No glory I covet," written by the Rev. Thomas Fitzgerald. The words of this latter are of the heavy, didactic character, in favour in the middle of the 18th century, but intolerable now. For this reason I have not given it ; also because it is not by any means the best of Whichello's compositions.

As an instance of the manner in which a heavy moralising song held its own, we may note that Captain Marryat puts this very song into the mouth of Old Tom the Lighterman, in "Jacob Faithful." Tom had lost his legs in the Battle of Trafalgar. He sang—

" No glory I covet, no riches I want,
Ambition is nothing to me.
But one thing I beg of kind Heaven to grant—"

Whereupon young Tom's shrill treble chimes in—

" For breakfast a good cup of tea."

"Oh, forbear to bid me slight thee," is in Watt's "Musical Miscellany," vol. v. 1731.

Whichello was for some years deputy to Hart, as organist of the churches of St. Andrew Undershaft, and St. Michael's, Cornhill. He was afterwards elected organist to St. Edmund's. He composed many songs, which were at first engraved and issued separately, but several found their way into such collections as Watt's "Musical Miscellany." He died about the year 1745. "No glory I covet" is in the sixth volume of this collection, 1731, as well as three more ; and as many as eight of his compositions in the fifth volume. He is sometimes named Abiel, sometimes Abriell.

Aaron Hill's song was set to another tune by Battishill, and this appeared in "The Pianoforte Magazine," circ. 1790. Again it was set by Hummel in Charles Knight's "Vocal Library," circ. 1840.

Thro' all the Employments of Life (p. 106). The air is that of "The old woman clothed in grey," and this is the first ballad tune sung in the "Beggars' Opera," and to it is set Peachum's cynical song.

One evening, when the celebrated actress, Mrs. Pritchard, was staying in the country with her family, she went to a performance given in a barn by a strolling company. For orchestra there was but a single fiddler. Mrs. Pritchard laughed loudly, and ridiculed the acting, greatly disconcerting the poor performers. Some one whispered the fiddler who she was, whereupon he, turning round, looked her steadily in the face, and struck up, "Through all the Employments of Life." "Come, it is time to be gone," said Mrs. Pritchard, colouring, and starting up. "We are discovered, and that fiddler is a clever fellow."

She curtsied to the man, and thanked him for having rebuked her lack of taste and good feeling.

In "Old Ballads," 1726, the ballad, "An old woman clothed in grey," is given, and it is said that it is to be sung to the tune of "Kind husband and imperious wife." This song of "The kind husband but imperious wife" is found in the "Westminster Drollery," 1671, and in "Wit and Drollery," 1682.

A copy of "An old woman clothed in grey" is in Dr. Burney's collection of songs, with music, in the British Museum, and is dated 1662.

Another title for "An old woman clothed in grey" is "The Worcestershire wedding, or Joy and Sorrow."

It begins—

"An old woman clothed in grey,
Her daughter was charming and young,
Who chanced to be noodled away
By Roger's false flattering tongue."

It is a ballad that could not be reproduced, from its length and its coarseness.

The tune is found in another form, as "Let Oliver now be forgotten." The difference is due merely to the accommodating of the original air to a metre which it would not fit in its pristine form. Any one familiar with the ways of old song-men in country places at the present day will know how that they thus alter and adapt airs to metres which one would have thought impossible to be sung to them.

The air in this new form is also called "How unhappy is Phillis in love." Both words and music of "Let Oliver now be forgotten," are contained in "180 Loyal Songs," 1685 and 1694 ; also in "Pills to Purge Melancholy," 1719. This song begins—

"Let Oliver now be forgotten,
His policy quite out of doors ;
Let Bradshaw and Hewson lie rotten,
Like sons of, &c.
For Tony grown a patrician
By voting damned sedition—
For many years
Fam'd politician,
The mouth of all Presbyter-Peers."

The reference is, of course, to the infamous Anthony Ashley-Cooper, Earl of Shaftesbury. I have added a verse to the song, as there is but one in the original.

Adieu to Old England, adieu! (p. 108).—A song from "Vocal Music, or, The Songster's Companion," circ. 1778, vol. iv. This begins—

"Ye frolicsome sparks of the game,
Ye misers both wretched and old,
Come listen to Billy, my name,
Who once had his hat full of gold."

NOTES TO SONGS

The chorus to this is—

> "Then why should we quarrel for riches,
> Or any such glittering toys?
> A light heart and a thin pair of breeches,
> Go through the world, brave boys!"

But this chorus belongs to a much earlier song that is in "Perseus and Andromeda," which was acted at Drury Lane in 1728. The song thus runs—

> "How pleasant a sailor's life passes,
> Who roams o'er the watery main;
> No treasure he ever amasses,
> But cheerfully spends all his gain."

Then a parody, entitled "The Contented Parson," appeared to the same air. It begins—

> "I am a country parson,
> My living's twice ten pound a year;
> I have a mare to ride on,
> No troubles in life I fear."

There is a song I have come upon repeatedly, for the last ten years, as a folk-ballad in the West of England, that goes over the same ground as the song in "Vocal Music," but has more verses, and the chorus, "Adieu to Old England, adieu," in place of that from "Perseus and Andromeda."

The song from "Perseus and Andromeda" is found so late as 1817 in "The British Orpheus," Stockport.

The reader of Smollet may recollect that in "Roderick Random" the old uncle is represented as saying to his nephew, in 1736, "Come, my boy, don't be cast down; you shall go to sea with me. A light heart and a thin pair of breeches goes through the world, brave boys, as the song goes, eh!"

Air in "Perseus and Andromeda."

In "Vocal Music" the chorus to "Ye frolicksome sparks," is a mere repetition of the last two lines of each verse. I have therefore adopted the chorus of the folk-song as now sung. The folk-chorus, "Adieu to Old England, adieu," will perhaps be more acceptable than that which insists on a "Thin pair of breeches;" and the folk-melody of the chorus is also good, and better than a mere repetition.

In Infancy our Hopes and Fears (p. 110).—From the opera of "Artaxerxes" (1761), by Dr. Arne. In an interesting communication by Mr. W. H. Cummings to *The Musical Times* of Jan. 1, 1896, he says: "Arne's one object and motive in life seems to have been self-indulgence and self-glorification. He pretended to despise Purcell and Handel. Whether he really did so, or whether he acted purely from jealousy when he attempted to detract from their merits, is a moot point. My own opinion inclines to the latter suggestion, for it seems impossible that such an excellent musician should have been deaf and blind to the greatness of his predecessor, Purcell, and his contemporary, Handel. . . . In 1770 Garrick produced at Drury Lane Theatre an *improved* and *revised* version of Dryden's 'King Arthur,' and doubtless at that time Arne was regarded as the most accomplished theatre musician; it was therefore quite natural that Garrick should consult him as to the possibility of including Purcell's music, originally written for the play, in the revival. Bearing in mind what has been said of Arne's character, it will not perhaps create much surprise to read the letter here given, which he addressed to Garrick:—

"'SIR,—A due attention to your commission having gone hand in hand with what fancy and judgment I may be thought to possess in my profession, I thought it necessary to lay before you a true state of the merits and demerits of the musical performance you are about to exhibit in King Arthur. To attain a certain rectitude, in judging of this matter, I have not only, with the utmost care and candor, inspected the score of Purcell's composition, but attended two rehearsals of it, the result of which is as follows:—

"The long scene of the Sacrifice, in the 1st Act, necessary to be deliver'd in, as being written, for music, may have a solemn and noble effect provided that the last Air and chorus, "I call you all to Wodenhall," be perform'd, as I have new compos'd it; the introductory Air to be sung by Champnes, which, being highly spirited, will carry off, with an *eclát*, an (otherwise) dull, tedious, antiquated suite of chorus: Besides which, that song, as set by Purcell, is intirely out of Mrs. Baddely's compass, very indifferent, and no way proper for a woman, where a troop of warriors are assembled, to bribe their Idols, for Success in battle.

"'The following song and chorus—"Come, if you dare, our Trumpets sound," is, in Purcell, tolerable; but so very short of that Intrepity and spirited defiance pointed at by Dryden's words and sentiments, that, I think, you have only to hear what I have compos'd, on the occasion, to make you immediately reject the other.

"'The air, "Let not a Moon-born Elf mislead you," after the two first bars of Purcell, very bad, and out of Mrs. Champnes' compass of voice. Hear mine. All the other solo songs of Purcell are infamously bad—so very bad, that they are privately the objects of sneer and ridicule to the musicians, but I have not meddled with any that are not to come from the mouths of your principal Performers. I wish you wou'd only give me leave to *Doctor* this performance.—I would certainly make it pleasing to the Public, which otherwise may prove an obstruction to the success of the Revival.—It is not *now* my intention to new set many things, mention'd in our original plan; but to put it in the power of your principal performers to make a proper figure, by opening and adorning the most entertaining points of view, wherein *they* are to *appear*; consequently, the expense will be much short of the sume propos'd; all self-interest subsiding to the earnest desire I shall ever entertain of proving my sincerity.'

"I stile my self — Sr.
Your devoted humble Sr.
= Thos Auge Arne

NOTES TO SONGS

"Artaxerxes was the first play Charles Lamb saw enacted, and I may be excused quoting his account of it as he saw it when 'not past six years old.'

"'I had dabbled a little in the "Universal History"—the ancient part of it—and here was the Court of Persia. It was being admitted to a sight of the past. I took no proper interest in the action going on, for I understood not its import; but I heard the word Darius, and I was in the midst of Daniel. All feeling was absorbed in vision. Gorgeous vests, gardens, palaces, princesses passed before me. I knew not players. I was in Persopolis for the first time, and the burning idol of their devotion almost converted me into a worshipper. I was awe-struck, and believed these significations to be something greater than elemental fires. It was all enchantment and a dream. No such pleasure has since visited me, but in dreams.'

"Returning to the theatre after an interval of some years, he vainly looked for the same feelings to recur with the same occasion. He was disappointed. 'At the first period I knew nothing, understood nothing, discriminated nothing. I felt all, loved all, wondered all —"was nourished I could not tell how." I had left the temple a devotee, and was returned a rationalist. The same things were there materially; but the emblem, the reference was gone!'

"It is clear that the musical faculty was nowhere, of no account in Charles Lamb. As a child of six he was all eye; had the other gift been in him, he would have been all ear, and the enchantment of the latter stage would have been equal to, greater than that of the first."

Cast, my Love, thine Eyes (p. 112).—A delicately lovely duet or dialogue, between Damon and Floretta, in "The Harlequin Sorcerer," 1752. It appears in "Clio and Euterpe," 1759, vol. i. p. 12, and is by Dr. Arne. It found its way into "The Syren," 1764; "S. Cecilia," 1782; "The Vocal Enchantress," 1782; and many other song-books. The "Harlequin Sorcerer" was an old piece that was revived with Arne's music, see *Gentleman's Magazine*, February 1752. The duet was sung by Lowe and Mrs. Lampe.

The music to the original pantomime was by Galliard, and appeared in 1725; but this duet was added on the reproduction of the piece twenty-seven years after.

My Dog and I (p. 118).—This song exists in two forms. One begins—

"Lavender's green, lavender's blue,
You must love me, 'cause I love you;
I heard one say, since I came hither,
That you and I must wed together.

My hostess's maid, her name was Nell,
She was a lass that I loved well;
But if she die, by some mishap,
Then she shall lie under the tap,

That she may drink when she is dry,
Because she loved my dog and I.
Call up your maids, set them to work,
Some to make hay, some to the rock (spindle).

James at the George, Sue at the Swan,
He loves his maid, she loves her man;
But, if they chance for to be found,
Catch them i' th' corn, put them i' th' pound.

I heard a bird sing in my ear,
'Maids will be scarce the next new year;
For young men are so wanton grown
That they ne'er mind which is their own.'"

The whole of this is interspersed with "Daddle-daddle." It is in black-letter, and the date is between 1672 and 1685.
This had its own air, "Lavender's green," portions of it still remaining in the nursery as a jingle sung to children. The complete ballad is in the edition, by Chappell & Ebsworth, of the "Roxburghe Ballads," iv. p. 434.

The other song on the same lines begins—

"You that are of the merry throng,
Give good attention to my song;
I'll give you weighty reasons why,
'Tis made upon my dog and I.
   My dog and I, my dog and I,
   'Tis made upon my dog and I.

I of no dogged nature am,
But loving, gentle, mild, and tame,
And have no larger family
Than only two, my dog and I."

The third verse begins, "I loved a maid, her name was Nell" (see "George Ridler's Oven," p. x.), and this song consists of seventeen stanzas. One has reference to Prince Rupert—

"There was a time when rebel rant
Did fear Prince Rupert and his days."

This song was to be sung to its own tune, "My Dog and I," or to "Bobbing Joan." We give a cento from this ballad to the tune of "Bobbing Joan" which is found in every edition of "The Dancing-Master," and in "Musick's Delight on the Cithren," 1666. It occurs in several of the ballad operas—in "Polly," 1729; in "The Bays' Opera," 1730; "The Mad Hour," 1737; "A Cure for a Scold," 1738.

The tune is mentioned as "a new Bob-in-Jo" in the "Mercurius Democritus," December 1652; and D'Urfey, in one of his songs, says—

"Then plump Bobbing Joan straight called for her own,
And thought she frisk'd better than any,
Till Sisly, with pride, took the fiddler aside,
And bade him strike up 'Northern Nanny.'"
—"Pills to Purge Melancholy" (1719), ii. p. 232.

Hope told a flattering Tale (p. 121).—This song was first published in a "Select Collection of Songs by Corri, arranged by Paesiello," vol. iv., *circ.* 1795. The words were by "Peter Pindar," *i.e.,* Dr. Walcot. It seems to have had an Italian origin to the words, "A che nel Pettoio sento." It was introduced by Madame Mara into "Artaxerxes," and rearranged by Mazzinghi in 1795, and printed and published by Goulding. It was again republished by Walker in 1805. In Hyde's "Collection," 1798, the song is attributed to Signor Paesiello. It appeared in Sibbald's "Vocal Magazine," vol. iii. 1799, and has become a stock English song; it is very generally, but erroneously, attributed to Dr. Arne, on account of the introduction into "Artaxerxes."

INDEX TO SONGS—Vol. VI.

*** In cases where the First Line differs from the Title, the former is also given (in italics). The figures in parentheses refer to the page at which the NOTE will be found.

A Cheshire Man sail'd unto Spain (vi.)	72
Adieu to Old England (xi.)	108
Adieu to the Village Delights (xi.)	102
Advice to the Fair Sex (v.)	49
As I saw Fair Clora walk (viii.)	88
BANKS of Allan Water, The (vii.)	77
Begone, Dull Care (ii.)	20
Bound Prentice to a Waterman (iv.)	42
CAST, my Love, Thine Eyes (xiii.)	112
Cheshire Cheese, The (vi.)	72
DIVER, The (vi.)	64
ENCOMPASSED by an Angel's Frame (viii.)	86
GATHER your Rosebuds whilst ye may (ii.)	16
George Ridler's Oven (x.)	100
Give that Wreath to me (ii.)	11
HAPPY Land! (ii.)	8
He Comes from the Wars (iii.)	34
Here's a Health to the Lass (v.)	60
Here's a Health unto His Majesty (iii.)	28
Hope told a Flattering Tale (xiii.)	121
I AM a Poor Shepherd Undone (ii.)	14
I Dreamt that I Dwelt in Marble Halls (v.)	54
If Torn from Thee (iii.)	24
I have a Silent Sorrow (vi.)	68
I lov'd a Maid, Her Name was Nell (xiii.)	118
In Infancy our Hopes and Fears (xii.)	110
In the Caverns Deep of the Ocean Cold (vi.)	64
I pray Thee send me back my Heart (vii.)	84
JEWEL is my Lady Fair, A (v.)	46
Last Valentine Day (ii.)	22
Let Ambition Fire thy Mind (v.)	62
Let me Wander not Unseen (ix.)	96
Long, Long Ago (viii.)	92
Love will Find out the Way (iii.)	32

MERMAID, The (vi.)	74
Miller of Dee, The (iii.)	30
My Dog and I (xiii.)	118
My Father in Leather was Clad (xi.)	108
No Flower that Blows (vii.)	80
OH! Forbear to bid me Slight Her (xi.)	104
Oh, Pilot, 'tis a Fearful Night (v.)	57
Old Ringwood (ix.)	94
On Friday Morn when we set Sail (vi.)	74
On the Banks of Allan Water (vii.)	77
Over the Mountains and over the Waves (iii.)	32
PHILLIS on the New-Mown Hay (vi.)	70
Pilot, The (v.)	57
REST, Warrior, Rest (iii.)	34
SHEPHERDS, have you Seen my Pastora (v.)	52
Softly Rise, O Southern Breeze (iv.)	37
Somebody (v.)	44
Stammering Lovers, The (ii.)	22
Sweet Smells the Briar (i.)	4
Tell me the Tales (viii.)	92
There is a Flower that Bloometh (i.)	1
There was a Jolly Miller (iii.)	30
The Stones that built George Ridler's Oven (x.)	100
They Tell us that You Mighty Powers (ix.)	98
Through all the Employments of Life (xi.)	106
'Twas on a Pleasant Summer's Day (i.)	6
WELL-A-DAY! (i.)	6
Were I oblig'd to Beg my Bread (v.)	44
When Lubin Sings of Youth's Delight (ii.)	18
When the Shepherds Seek to Woo (v.)	49
Ye Darksome Woods, where Echo Dwells (ix.)	94

There is a Flower that Bloometh.

Words by E. FITZBALL. VINCENT WALLACE. (W. H. H.)

E. VI. a.

Sweet Smells the Briar.

Words by E. SPENSER.

Music by JOHN PERCY.
(H. F. S.)

5

rall.

| s :l .t | s :— .d¹ | d¹ .t :d¹ .l | t : | s :l .t | d¹ :t | d¹ .m :s .f| s :— |

For could we care - less enter pleasures bow'r, Then pleasure would re-sign her noblest ends.

p　　　　　　　　　　　　　　*f*　　*rall.*　　*ad lib.*

a tempo　　　　　　　　　　　　　　*rall.*

| l :s .,f | m :— .f | s .,s :f. m | r : | d¹ : t .l | d¹ .d :d .f | m :r | d :— |

Why then should I think much of trifling pain? Which end-less pleasure shall un - to me gain.

p a tempo　　　　　　　*p*　　*f*　　*rall.*

p a tempo　　　　　　　*cres.*

| m :r ,d | d :d¹ | l ,f :s .l | s : | d¹ :d¹ ,l | t :s | l ,s :l .t | s : |

Sweet smells the briar but, touch'd, a - vows its scorn; Sweet is the cy-press, but at - tun'd to woe;

p a tempo

cres.　　　　　　　　　*dim. e rall.*

| m :r .,d | d¹ :d¹ | l ,s :f .m | f :s | t .d¹,t:l .s | d¹ .d :l ,f | m :r | d :— |

Sweet is the rose, but arm'd with many a thorn; And sweet the vine but frenzies with it flow.

p　　　　　　　*cres.*　　　　　*dim. e rall.*

WELL-A-DAY!

2. All thro' the afternoon till eve,
   This shepherd did not cease to grieve,
       But played his notes forlorn;
   And still the theme he could not leave,
       Well-a-day!
           His plaintive lute sighed Well-a-day!

3. Were I the maid for whom he pin'd
   To pity I would be inclined,
       Nor treat him with such scorn;
   But me he loves not vex'd I find.
       Well-a-day!
           So now must I sing Well-a-day!

Words by J. BRUTON. Music by E. F. RIMBAULT.
(W. H. H.)

GIVE THAT WREATH TO ME.

Words by T. H. BAYLEY.

Old English Air, Arranged by Sir J. STEVENSON. (W. H. H.)

I am a poor Shepherd undone.

Old English
(H. F. S.)

15

Gather ye Rose-buds.

Words by R. HERRICK.
Music by WILLIAM LAWES.
(F. W. B.)

Ga-ther ye rose - buds whilst ye may, Old Time is still a - fly - ing,
That age is best which is the first, When youth and blood are warm - er,

And that same flow'r that smiles to - day, To - mor - row may be dy - ing.
But be - ing spent, to worse and worst, Times still suc - ceed the form - er.

E. VI. b.

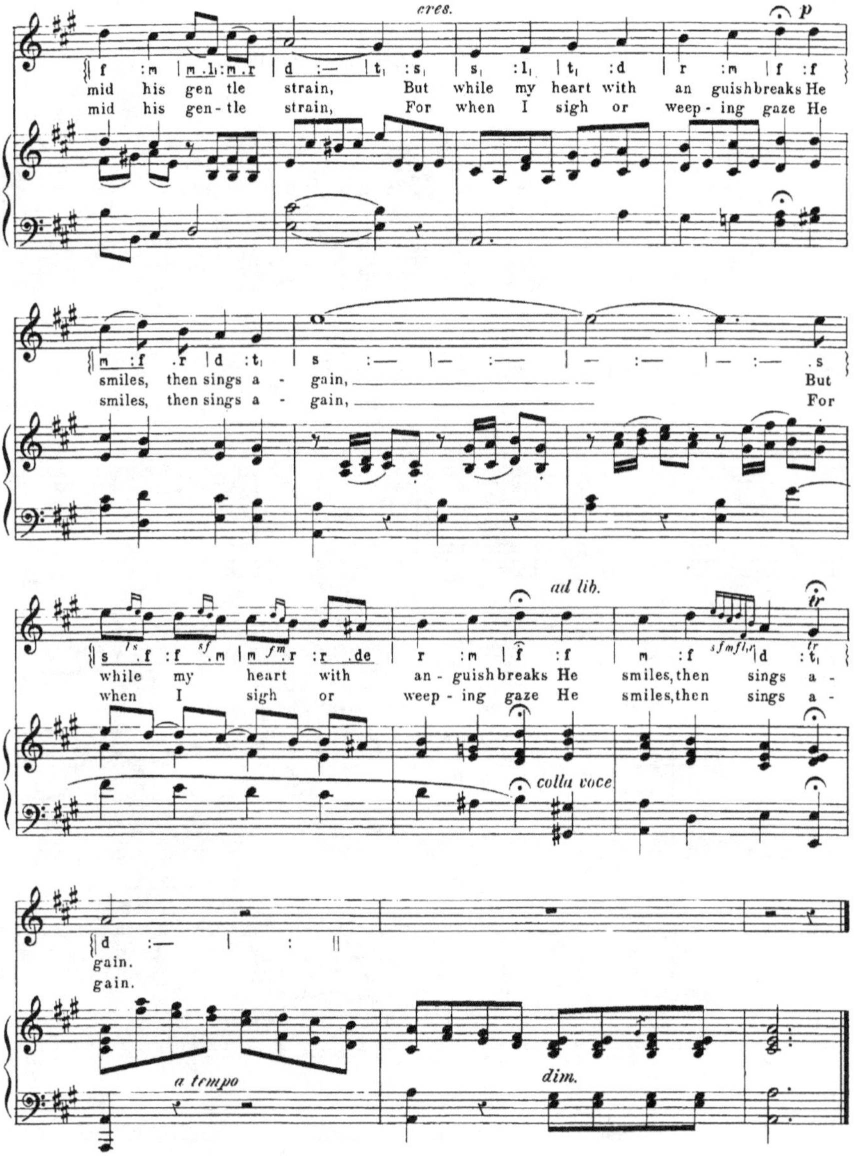
cres.
p
f :m |m.l,:m.r | d :— | t, :s, | s, :l, | t, :d | r :m | f :f
mid his gen tle strain, But while my heart with an guish breaks He
mid his gen-tle strain, For when I sigh or weep-ing gaze He
m :f .r | d :t, | s :— | — :— | — :— | — :— .s
smiles, then sings a - gain, But
smiles, then sings a - gain, For
ad lib.
tr
s .f :f .m | m .r :r .de | r :m | f :f | m :f | d :t,
while my heart with an - guish breaks He smiles, then sings a -
when I sigh or weep - ing gaze He smiles, then sings a -
colla voce
d :— | :
gain.
gain.
a tempo
dim.

BEGONE! DULL CARE.

17th Century.
(W. H. H.)

The Stammering Lovers.

Ancient Folk Song in the Dorian Mode.
(H.F.S.)

3.

I cannot tell how concluded was the matter,
   For shortly further they did go,
But how one did kick (stutter) and t'other did stammer,
   I laugh'd till my sides were sore, I trow,
O it made me laugh, laugh, la, la, la, la, laugh, laugh,
   As these lovers stood a-talking,
O it made me laugh, laugh, la, la, la, la, laugh, laugh,
   Abroad as I was a-walking.

If Torn From Thee.

HANDEL. From the Opera "Amadigi."
(H. F. S.) 1715.

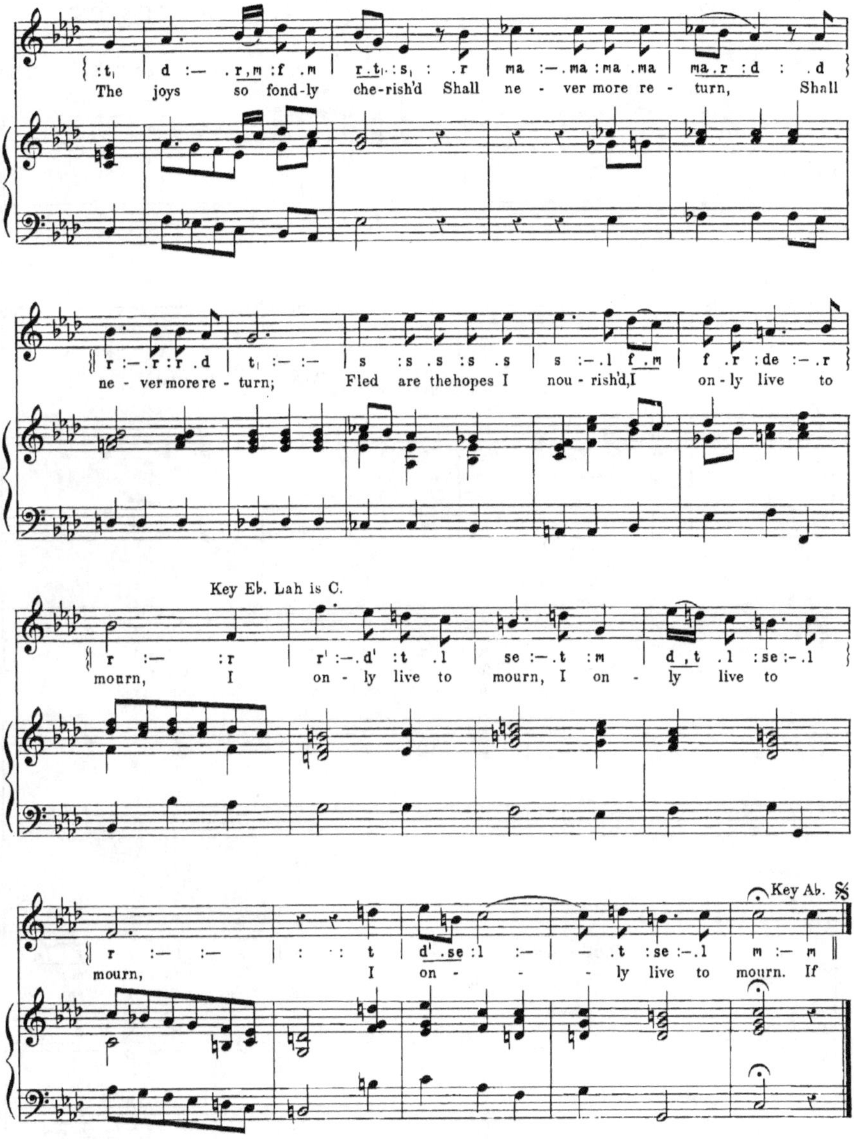
The joys so fond-ly che-rish'd Shall ne - ver more re - turn, Shall
ne - ver more re - turn; Fled are the hopes I nou - rish'd, I on - ly live to
Key E♭. Lah is C.
mourn, I on - ly live to mourn, I on - ly live to
Key A♭.
mourn, I on - - - ly live to mourn. If

HERE'S A HEALTH UNTO HIS MAJESTY.

J. SAVILE. (W. H. H.)

THE MILLER OF DEE.

Old English.
(W. H. H.)

Rest, Warrior, Rest.

MICHAEL KELLY.
(W. H. H.)

Softly rise, O southern breeze.

Aria from "Solomon, a Serenata."

Dr W. BOYCE. 1743.
(H. F. S.)

38

BOUND PRENTICE TO A WATERMAN.

J. SANDERSON.
(W. H. H.)

3.

With Drake I've sail'd the world around and learn'd a bit to fight,
But somehow I a prisoner was ta'en;
So when the Spanish jailor to my dungeon show'd a light,
I blinded both his peepers, and then ran away again,
Singing, &c.

4.

I've run many risks in life, on ocean and on shore,
But always like a Briton got the day;
And fighting in Old England's cause I will as many more
But let me face ten thousand foes, will never run away,
Singing, &c.

SOMEBODY.

Composer unknown.
(W. H. H.)

3.

But should I ever live to see
That form be mine, now loved by me,
Then thou'lt reward my constancy,
And I'll be blest with somebody.
My own dear somebody, my constant somebody,
Then shall my tears be dried by thee,
And I'll be blest with somebody.

A JEWEL IS MY LADY FAIR.

H. PURCELL.
(W. H. H.)

Advice to the Fair Sex.

Composer Unknown.
(F. W. B.)

Shepherds, have you seen my Pastora.

I DREAMT THAT I DWELT IN MARBLE HALLS.

Words by ALFRED BUNN.

Music by M. W. BALFE.
(W. H. H.)

Andantino.

Piano. *dolce assai*

pp

Key E♭.

| :s | s......:d' :t | s :t :l | s :l :s | m :— :m |

1. I dreamt that I dwelt in mar - ble halls, With
2. I dreamt that sui - tors sought my hand; That

vas - sals and serfs at my side, ——— And of all who as-
knights up - on bend - - ed knee, ——— And with vows no

sem-bled with - in those walls, That I was the hope and the
maid - en's heart could with - stand, They pledg'd their faith to

pride. ——— I had rich - es too great to count; could
me. ——— And I dreamt that one of that no - ble

boast Of a high an - ces - tral name. ——— But I
host Came forth my hand to claim. ———

The Pilot.

Words by T. H. BAYLEY. S. NELSON. (W. H. H.)

3.

"On such a night the sea engulf'd
My father's lifeless form:
My only brother's boat went down
In just as wild a storm;
And such, perhaps, may be my fate,
But still I say to thee,
Fear not, but trust in Providence
Wherever thou may'st be."

Here's a Health to the Lass.

3.
For the fellow that findeth an honest maid
Of naught in the world need he be afraid,
Out of nothing at all he is something made,
  So it ever has been since life began.

4.
I warrant that man were in doleful plight,
He'd wander agaping from day till night,
'Tis the function of woman to set him right,
  Of the hobble dehoy to make the man.

LET AMBITION FIRE.
Tenor Song.

Words by W. CONGREVE.

Music by WELDON.
(F. W. B.)

2.
Crowns I'll lay beneath thy feet,
　Thou on necks of kings shall tread;
Joys, encircling joys shall meet,
　Which way e'er thy fancy leads.

3.
Let not toil of empire fright,
　Toils of empire pleasures are;
Thou shalt only know delight,
　All the joy and not the care.

4.
Shepherd, if thou yield'st the prize
　For the blessings I bestow,
Joyful I'll ascend the skies,
　Happy shalt thou reign below.

The Diver.

G. DOUGLAS THOMPSON.
E. J. LODER.
(W. H. H.)

I HAVE A SILENT SORROW HERE.

Words by R. B. SHERIDAN.

Music by GEORGINA, Duchess of Devonshire.
(W. H. H.)

Phillis on the New-Mown Hay.

Old English.
(H. F. S.)

Phil - lis on the new-mown hay, Fair but lone - ly still she lay,
Told her he had lov'd her long, Lov'd her well and lov'd her strong;

3.
He had bought the wedding ring,
Many a bow and silken string,
Fit for any Queen or King,
To shew he truly loved her;
Thus did he declare and sing,
Until at last he moved her.

THE CHESHIRE CHEESE.

Folk Song.
(W. H. H.)

3.
The Cheshire man ran to his hold,
And fetched a Cheshire cheese;
And said, "Look here, you dog, behold!
We have such fruits as these.

4.
"Your fruits mature but twice a year,
As you yourself did say;
But such as I you offer here,
Our land gives twice a day."

5.
The Spaniard in a fury flew,
His rapier took in hand;
The Cheshire man kick'd up his heels
With "Sir! at your command."

6.
So never let a Spaniard boast
While Cheshire men abound;
Lest they should teach him to his cost
To dance a Cheshire round.

74

THE MERMAID.

Folk Song (H. F. S.)

Boldly and Cheerfully.

Key D. {:m .,f | s :— .,m | s :— .,l | s :s .,m | s :s .,l | s .,f :m .,r | d :s .,s | l :f | d' :t .,l | s : l :l .,t }

On Fri- day morn when we set sail, And our ship not far from the land; We
Then up spoke the captain of our gal-lant ship, And a brave young man was he; I've a

3.

Then up and spake the little cabin boy,
And a pretty little boy was he;
O! I'm more grieved for my daddy and my mam
Than you for your wife may be.
   For raging seas, did roar, &c.

4.

Then three times round went our gallant ship,
And three times round went she;
For the want of a life boat all went down,
And she sank to the bottom of the sea,
   For raging seas did roar, &c.

The Banks of Allan Water.

Words by M. G. LEWIS.

Composer unknown
(W. H. H.)

NO FLOWER THAT BLOWS.

From the Opera of "Selima and Azor."
T. LINLEY.
(W. H. H.)

Allegretto moderato.

I PRAY THEE SEND ME BACK MY HEART.

Words by Sir JOHN SUCKLING. Music by ED. MILLER, Mus. Doc.
(H. F. S.)

Encompassed by an Angel's Frame.

W. JACKSON, (Exeter.)
(W. H. H.)

LONG, LONG AGO.

Words and Music by T. HAYNES BAYLY.
(W. H. H.)

3.

Though by your kindness my fond hopes were raised,
    Long, long ago, long, long ago;
You, by more eloquent lips have been praised,
    Long, long ago, long ago.
But by long absence your truth has been tried,
Still to your accents I listen with pride,
Blest as I was when I sat at your side
    Long, long ago, long ago.

OLD RINGWOOD.

Words by R. BLOOMFIELD. W. HAWES. (W. H. H.)

3.
The charming notes of cheerful hounds,
Hark! how the hollow dale resounds,
   The sunny hills how gay!
But where's the note, brave dog, like thine?
Then urge the steed! the chorus join!
   'Tis Ringwood leads the way.

LET ME WANDER NOT UNSEEN.

Words by MILTON.

Music by HANDEL.
(H. F. S.)

Siciliana. Key F. Lah is D.

Let me wan-der not un-seen By hedgerow Elms on hil-locks green, There the plough-man near at hand Whis-tles o'er the fur-row'd

They tell us that you mighty powers.
Song in The Indian Queen.

Words by Sir ROBERT HOWARD. Music by HENRY PURCELL.
(H. F. S.)

GEORGE RIDLER'S OVEN.

Gloucestershire Folk Song.
(W. H. H.)

5.
When I'd three sixpences 'neath my thumb,
O welcome everywhere was I;
But where I'd none, I might not come,
'Tis poverty parts good company.

Adieu to the Village Delights.

BAILDON.
(W. H. H.)

103

Key B♭
Lah is G.

{ d :- :- :- | :ˢ,r | t₁:d t₁ :l.s₁ | d :d :r | m :- :- | - :- :r | d :f :m }
void.___ A-dieu thou sweet health-breathing hill!___ Thou canst not my
died.___ Her eyes that so beau-ti-ful shone___ Are clos-ed for

{ m.r :d :t₁ | l₁:- :- |- :- :r.d.t₁,l | s₁:-.l₁ :s₁ | m :r :d | t₁:- :- | - :- :d }
com-fort re-store,___ For ev-er a-dieu, my dear rill,___ My
ev-er in sleep,___ And mine since my Lu-cy is gone___ Have

{ r :d :t | d :-.r :m | m :r : | :d :d | d :- :- | - :- :- | - :- :d }
Lu-cy, a-las! is no more, is no more,___ no
no-thing to do but to weep, but to weep,___ to

rall.
{ d :t₁ :r | m :-.r :d | t₁.l₁.s₁.f₁ m₁:r₁ | :s₁ | s₁:- :- :- : }
         d₁:- :- :- : }
more My Lu-cy, a-las! is no more.
weep Have no-thing to do but to weep.
colla voce

Through all the Employments of Life.

Words (1st verse) by J. GAY.
Old English. (H. F. S.)

With animation, but not too fast.

Key B♭
Lah is G.

1. Through all the em-ploy-ments of life, Each neighbour a-bus-es his brother: Fault find-ing 'twixt hus-band and wife, All pro-
2. But sure-ly some hon-es-ty lies In each who the o-ther one blames; And ro-gue-ry 'scap-eth his eyes, In him-

Adieu to Old England.

2.
My fortune is pretty well spent,
　My lands and my cattle and corn;
I must put on a face of content
　When as naked as when I was born.
No more I'll be troubled with wealth,
　My pockets are drained full dry,
I walk where I please for my health,
　And never fear robbing, not I.
　　　So adieu, &c.

3.
O once I would eat of the best,
　The finest of bread that was white;
Now glad if a crust may be had
　And thankful to have it to bite.
And once I would drink of the best,
　The best of ale, humming and brown,
Now fain some clean water to gain
　That runneth from mountain or down.
　　　So adieu, &c.

4.
O once I could lie on the best,
　The best of good beds made of down,
If sure of a flock of dry straw
　I am glad to keep off the cold ground.
Some say, that old care kill'd the cat,
　And starv'd her for fear she should die.
Henceforth I'll be wiser than that,
　To my cares bid for ever good-bye.
　　　So adieu, &c.

In Infancy.

Dr ARNE.
(W. H. H.)

CAST, MY LOVE, THINE EYES.
Duet.

117

My Dog and I.

Old English
(F. W. B.)

Hope told a flattering tale.

Words by PETER PINDAR.   Composer unknown. 1795.
(H. F. S.)

www.ingramcontent.com/pod-product-compliance
Lightning Source LLC
Chambersburg PA
CBHW031323160426
43196CB00007B/635